Seriously good photography tips for camera phones

Contents

This is me .... page 2

Introduction .... page 4

1 The basics to get started .... page 6

2 Bad photography! .... page 7

3 Better photography .... page 8

4 Fill the frame .... page 9

5 Rule of thirds .... page 10

6 Use manual focus .... page 14

7 Background .... page 15

8 Eye level .... page 16

9 Stay steady .... page 17

10 Shoot in landscape mode .... page 18

11 Take two, three, four photos .... page 19

12 Do not use zoom. Ever .... page 20

13 Edit with subtlety! .... page 21

14 Use natural light .... page 22

15 Use flash outside! .... page 23

16 Get a better camera phone .... page 24

17 Back up images .... page 25

18 The End .... page 26

All images (except stated) © Copyright Garry Cook 2015
ISBN-13 978-1507504178
ISBN- 1507504179

This is me

Garry Cook

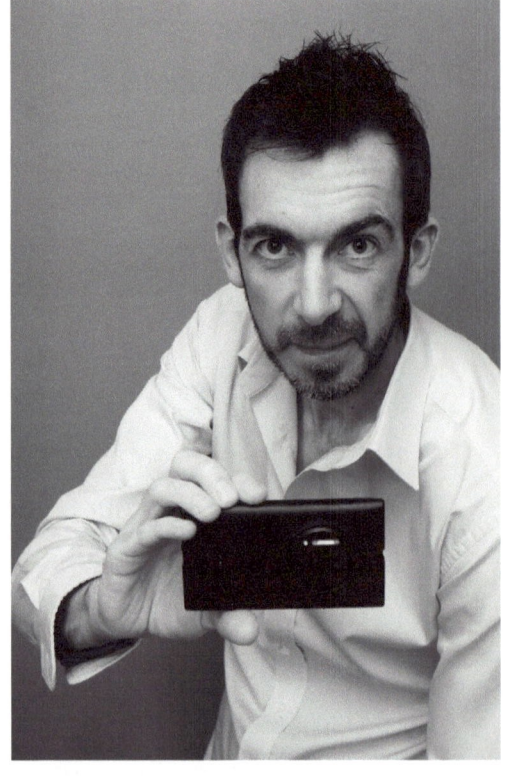

I am a writer and photographer.

I've written for most national newspapers in Britain, plus a few magazines, including Practical Photography and Photography Monthly.

I've also published a few documentary photography books. Some of my other books also include words. Such as the only humorous book on the troubles between Israel and Palestine: Palestiniana.

I was first asked to hold a series of mobile phone photography workshops when Trinity Mirror started handing out camera phones to their journalists, telling them: You take the photos now for your own stories.

This guide focuses less on editorial photography and more on general techniques. I've written it to help people take better photographs on their mobile phones*

Seriously good photography tips for camera phones

*The truth

I haven't really written this guide to help people take better photographs on their mobile phones.

I've written it because I'm sick of seeing really bad photography on Facebook and Twitter, taken by people who clearly do not know how to use their mobile phones.

But I do love it that almost everyone now carries a camera. The world is being documented like never before. We're viewing images taken in places we never used to get to see - though I'm not a fan of selfies in public toilets. I can tell you for a fact that mobile phone cameras were not invented for this.

Introduction

Terms and conditions

These are the terms I am about to use to push you to be a hugely talented, highly impressive photographer (with a mobile phone).

Subject: This refers to the main thing in your image. It can be a person, animal or object (dustbin, steam train, electricity pylon). I'm not here to judge you and your weird hobbies. I just want to make sure you take better photographs of your kids, cats or your kids with cats.

Editing: What is editing? Editing an image is when you change brightness, clarity, exposure colour levels etc in editing software, which will either come with the phone or on an app.

Mobile phone: American readers, this is a cell phone.

Extra note about ISO: I very briefly mention this term later (in America it is known as ASA). ISO refers to the light sensitivity of film. Film would typically be 100 IS0, 200 ISO 400 ISO 800 ISO etc. The higher the number, the better the film's ability to capture an image in poor lighting conditions. The trade off is the actual quality of the image, which degrades as the ISO number increases.

Seriously good photography tips for camera phones

Best quality images would be taken on 100 ISO film (or even 50 ISO). Rather bizarrely, this rating system was unnecessarily transferred to the first digital cameras - presumably to make it easier for converts to get to grips with the new technology.

Film sensitivity (ISO), along with shutter speed and aperture forms the trinity of variables which go to expose an image correctly. If you have a perfect exposure and change one of these three variables, the image will be affected in some way unless you change the others. Got it? Maybe a bit complicated but worth knowing. However, we shall be concentrating on simple photo techniques so don't really need to learn all this.

Conditions

There are no conditions, really. You can engage with me on Twitter @gazcook

You can ask questions on email: gazcook@hotmail.com

1

The basics

Wipe your lens. Phones in pockets = mucky lenses. Use a cloth or just your (clean) finger.

Next, technical stuff: Set the image resolution to highest possible in camera. Always take the best quality image you can, even if this means backing up images and removing them from your mobile phone's memory card more often because the file sizes are bigger.

Seriously good photography tips for camera phones

2 *Bad photography*

All press release images. Problems include: Lamppost out of head, flash reflection, door in background, poor exposure, boring certificates and wonkyness.

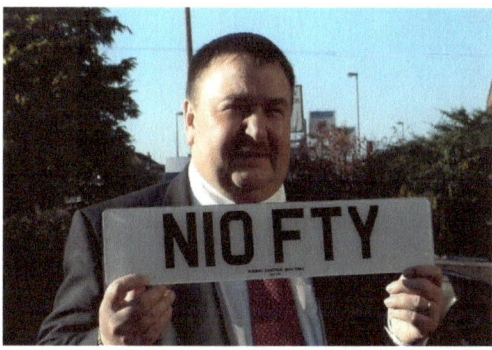

Lamppost out of head

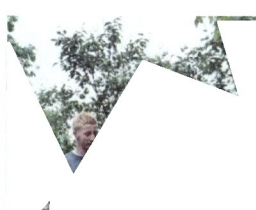

Poor exposure

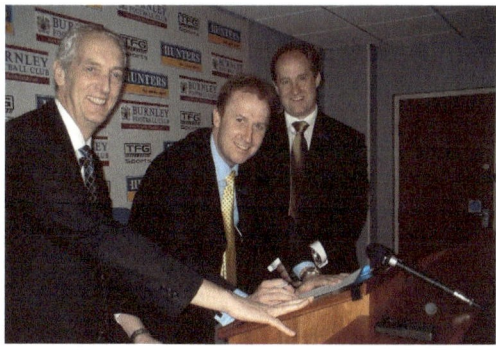

Distracting door in background (below) Boring, boring certificates

Flash reflection (below) Wonkyness

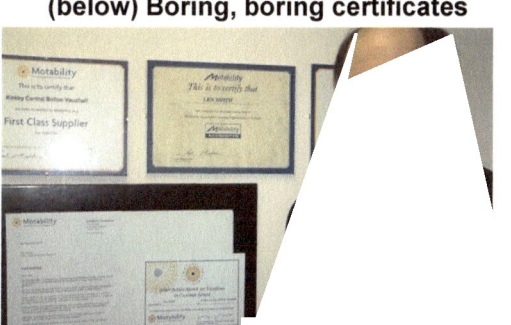

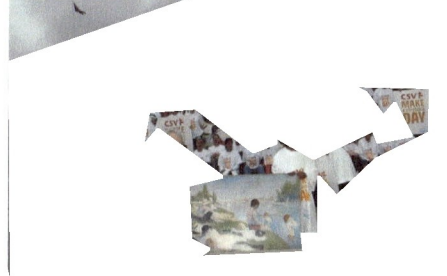

3

Better photography

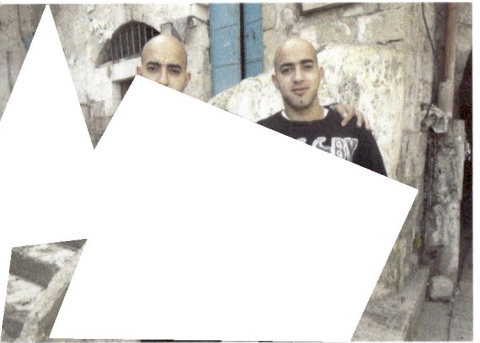

Fill the frame, symmetry, bodies only

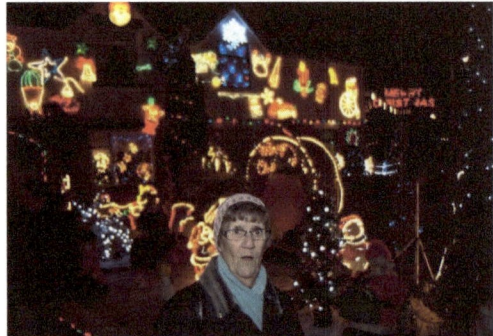

Breaking the rules of thirds

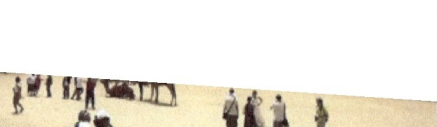

Rule of thirds, people giving scale
(below) Fill the frame

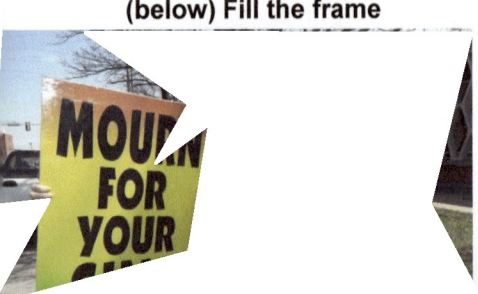

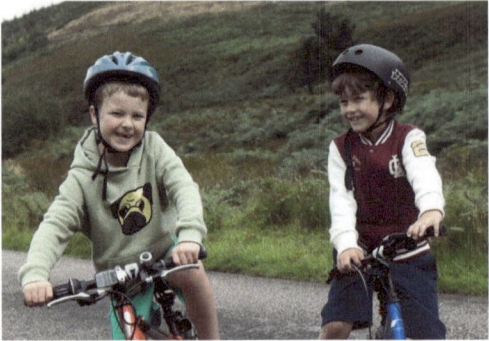

Fill the frame, at subject's eye level
(below) Natural framing

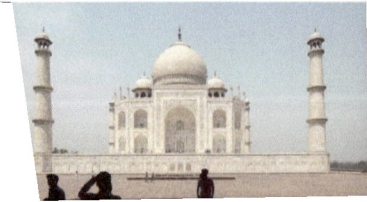

4

Fill the frame

The most important thing you can do to avoid Bad Photography.

It's the biggest mistake in photography - taking a photo from too far away.

Why does this happen? The photographer is scared of getting too close. Or they think that the photo should include the full body. Let's get one thing straight: full bodies in photographs are boring.

You will transform your photography if you get close to the subject. And while we're on the subject, head a shoulders shots look much better than full body poses.

If you are doing a photograph to gain publicity (for an event or a cause) and there is a group of people DO NOT photograph the entire group. Group shots are also dull, dull, dull. To make the photo more interesting, bring one person forward.

(below, left): Too many people, too far away. Boring.
(below, right): Focus on one person. Fill the frame. More impact.

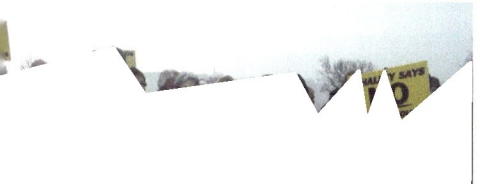

5

Rule of thirds

The rule of thirds is the most basic principle in photography.

Once you've embraced the idea to get closer to the subject, you need to know where to position them. Your subject can be a car, tree, person, red telephone box or your tortoise. It does not matter, the same principle applies (it's all based on science and nature).

And this is it:

Imagine this grid (below) across the image your are about to take. All you need to do is make sure the subject is roughly placed where any of the lines cross. There are four cross points. You only need to use one of them, though two is good.

This rule is so important in photography that some mobile phones have an on-screen grid option.

If you are photographing a person, you could get them to turn slightly into the image. This will often improve composition further.

This theory is actually based on science which we can see occur naturally in nature and in the universe. The rule of thirds is linked

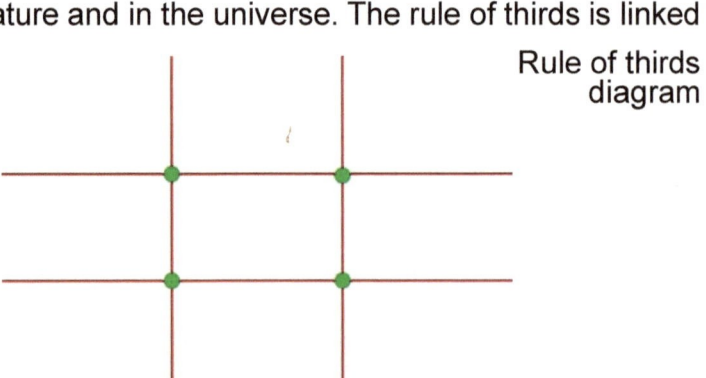

Rule of thirds
diagram

to the golden ratio, nautilus, the golden triangle and the Fibonacci numbers. Now, the science behind this is very complicated so, I've condensed it all down in to one very short sentence: All theories highlight the same four areas in an image and following this law makes a better photo.

There, that's all you need to know. Aesthetically, photographs work within this rule by giving the eye a starting point and a natural line to follow in to the image.

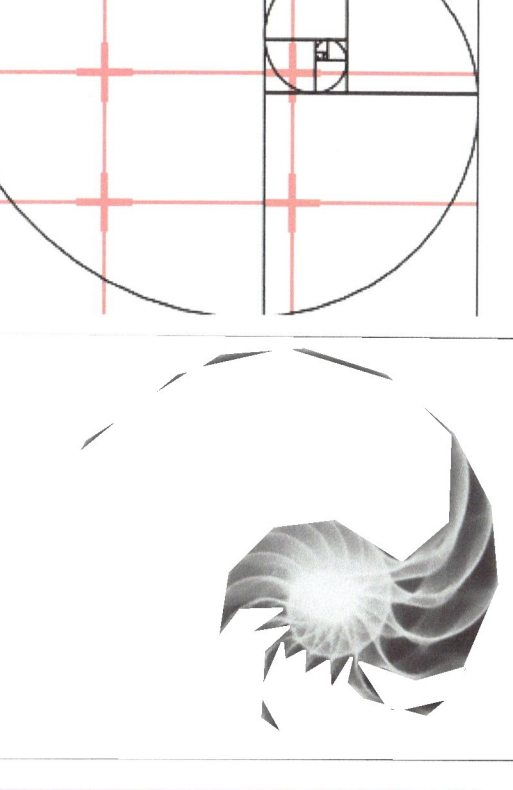

(diagram, top): The golden triangle on its own.

(right, top): See how the centre of the golden ratio is in roughly the same position as where two of the (red) rule of thirds lines cross.

The golden triangle grid *(below, right)* has lines meeting at the same area as the centre of the golden ratio curve.

Flip these diagrams around any way you like - the same four key areas apply (but you only need to use one of them).

Every time you see a decent photograph now, you will notice these key areas. The same applies to TV and film.

A nautilus marine mollusc shell
Nautilus: blog.lib.umn.edu/myee/architecture/

DON'T DO IT!

DO NOT: Take a photograph of a sunset, sea view or mountain. Very boring.
  UNLESS: You include some object in the foreground (on a rule-of-thirds point).
  ALSO: Get your subject (if a person) to turn slightly sideways into the image.

No rules

Rule of thirds

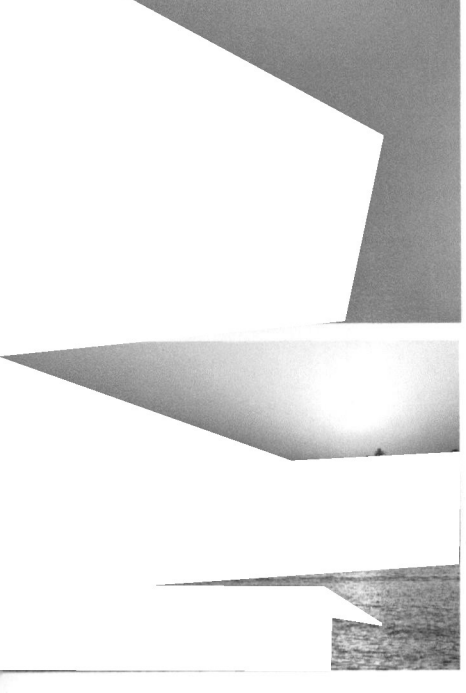
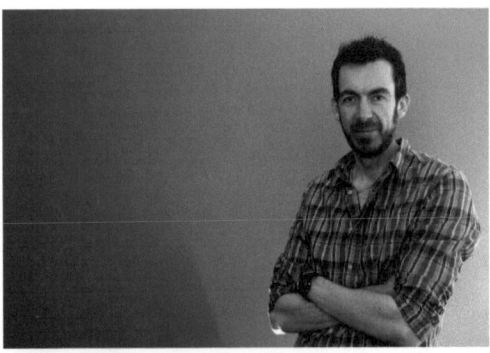
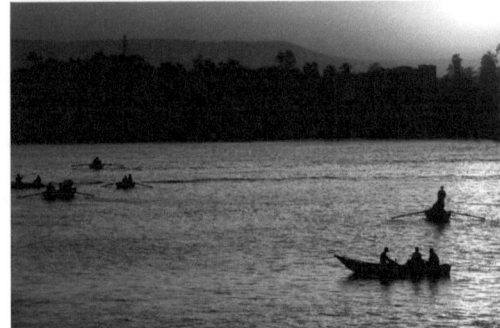

APPLYING THE RULE OF THIRDS

BAD PHOTOGRAPHS:
(Shown on the left here) Where either the eyes or horizion are dead centre of the image.

See all the wasted space around the head (to the top, left and right).

The photo is so much better if the eyes are level with the top horizontal line in the rule of thirds.

The image is also improved by having the body in line with one of the rule of thirds' vertical lines. And it's even better if you're closer to the subject.

The same rules apply to landscape photography (you can also have the horizon/waterline level with the lower horizonal line of the rule of thirds).

6

Use manual focus

Some of the better phones have manual focus as standard (where you can touch the screen and the lens focuses on that area). If your phone does not have this option, get an app which allows you to control focus.

Nokia (Windows) Lumia 1020 and iPhone 5S (and higher) allow manual focus and exposure.

Apps to try: **Camera+** (iPhone/Windows/Android)

Pro Camera 7 (iPhone/Android) £

Feeling confident?

Why not try adjusting exposure compensation?

All cameras expose an entire scene, based on an average scene (known as an 18percent gray card).

Don't worry about this. Too complicated. Just understand that if whatever your are taking a photo of has areas of high contrast (very bright or very dark areas) the camera's own calculation has a much higher risk of being wrong.

This means a badly exposed image. If you do it yourself, you could get better results. Takes practice.

If a photo, or areas within the photo, is too dark, expose + (plus). Too light? Then expose - (minus). This is a good one to experiment with if you've got a bit of time.

7

Background

Both press release images

Is the background cluttering up image?
This is what you need to avoid:
Fussy backgrounds (tree branches, lots of clashing colours, cars).
Lampposts. So easy to miss but so devastating when you get home, look at your photos and see the best shot is of someone with a stick coming out of their head.
And if you're using flash: avoid reflective surfaces (glass, mirrors) when using flash.
Also: In bright sunlight, don't take photos where someone's face is lit up while the rest of the scene is darker or in shadow. The camera will no be able to cope. Move the subject in to the shade if possible.

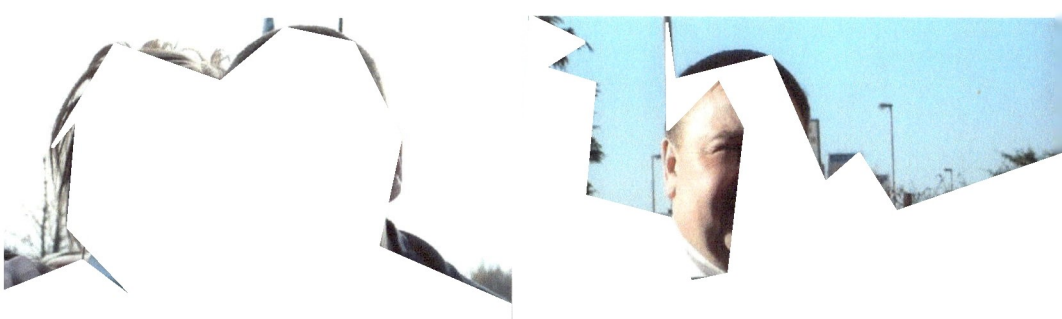

8

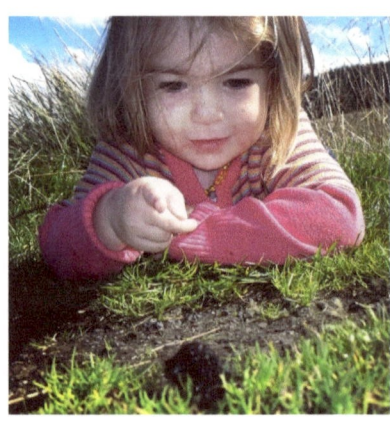

Eye level

Position your camera to your subject's eye level (if your subject is a living thing, with eyes). It's just laziness if you don't do this. And not so good for the creation of a beautiful image.

It's very easy to get out the camera, take a photo - and go home. Without thinking. But if you move down to eye level with your subject – particularly important with children, animals and very small people – you will dramatically improve the quality of your image. Especially if the subject looks directly in to the lens. That's into the lens, not at you. Or your waving hand.

And once you are comfortable with this technique, you can experiment for dramatic effect (very good if you're telling a story and trying to emphasise vulnerability or power):

High viewpoint looking down = subject looking vulnerable.
Low viewpoint looking up = subject looking powerful.

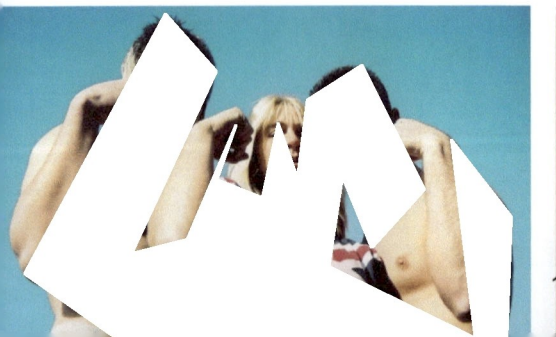

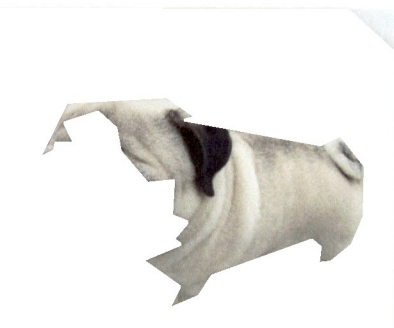

9

Stay steady

Be delicate. Work out how to press your shutter without shaking the phone.

If the phone actually moves when you press the shutter, consider yourself jittery. Try breathing out as you take a photo. And keep still for several moments. You know these mobile phones take a bit longer to take a photo, especially if there is a slower (longer) shutter speed because of low light.

A blurred image is bad enough. It means either you're no Steady Eddie or the person in the image was moving or running away.

But adding blur through an app or editing software is a bit of a gimmick. Usually looks a bit naff. Give this one swerve, I'm telling you.

The idea of adding blur to a photo is to add depth of field - the semi-technical term for throwing the background out of focus. With a decent lens on a big camera, this is quite easy to do - but only the best mobile phone cameras have this capability (and even then the effect is limited and sometimes difficult to control).

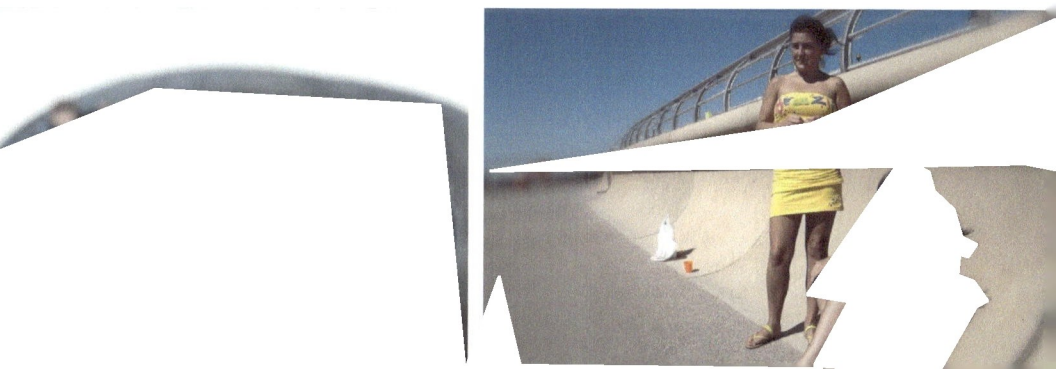

10

Shoot in landscape mode

Almost always shoot in landscape mode (this also applies to video). Portraits are best used (if you have to) just for one person, and even then only for head-and-shoulders shots. A full body portrait image is just awful*.

Portrait images look rubbish when uploaded to social media sites. If you insist on taking them, make sure they are in addition to landscape shots - not instead of. If a newspaper page designer wants to use a portarit shape image they can easily crop your lovely landscape shot.

*My opinion only. I've said this already.

11

Take two, three, four shots

Take several photos of the same set up? Are you serious? Well, yes. It's important. This is a safety routine because, as we already know, you're a bit jittery on that shutter button.

But you can't be blamed for people blinking, someone walking past in the background or a seagull flying through that beautiful piece of empty blue sky.

And once you've taken several images of a set up, try and alternative and do the same again. You will begin to learn what works and may be surprised at what turns out to be your most effective image.

12

Do not use zoom. Ever

Mobile phones and their lenses do not work well in zoom mode. Image quality is severely affected by using zoom. It's pretty much useless tool on every mobile phone camera, unless you're aim is to capture something very far off in a very grainy way. These are the photos you take on holiday and then never look at again because the quality is so bad.

It is much better to move closer to the subject and/or crop when editing the image later.

So I tell you this: Do not use zoom. Ever!

13

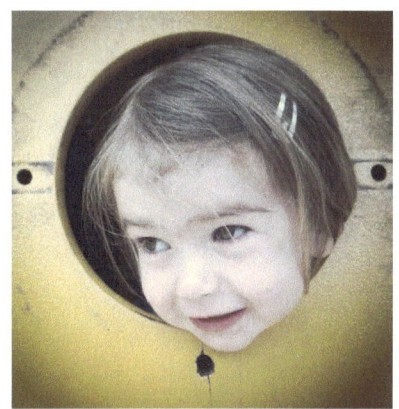

Edit delicately

So many camera phone images are too heavily manipulated. Heavy filters, over coloured, vignetting of corners. Yes, okay, sometimes these can look okay. But unless you add the same filters to every photo you take you will end up with a mish-mash of styles which does not look cool.

Editing does take longer, but the effect is usually better. Alter levels of vibrance (lower) and clarity (slightly higher) for instant improvements*. Also try brightness and reduce/increases shadows (if your editing software has that option).

If your image is taken indoors under artificial lighting, changing the white balance can improve the image.

When to use a filter: If a photo is taken in bad lighting.

Apps for editing images

Apps for editing images (if you can't do this with the software already installed on your phone):

Snapseed (iPhone/Android)
Adobe Photoshop Express (iPhone/Windows/Android)
Photoshop Touch (iPhone/ Android) £

Camera Awesome (iPhone/ Android) £ = Android only [this app includes option to overlay rule-of-thirds and golden ratio]
iPhoto (iPhone)
Instant improvements to most - but not all - images.

14

Use natural light

Most camera flashes, when used indoors, are not good enough. We've all seen those photos: subject lit okay, surrounding area just too dark. Not a very appealing image.

Often it is best to use natural light indoors. This will mean a longer shutter speed - which means increased chance of camera shake (anything exposure under 1/60sec can lead to blurred images) but on some camera phones set to automatic you will have no idea what exposure you camera is selecting. If you can move near a window to take the photo, the increased amount of light will help - as long as it is not direct sunlight shinning on to the subject.

If your mobile phone has the ability to set exposure/brightness/ISO/shutter speed levels in manual mode, you may be able to produce a good photo with flash. Otherwise, it's natural light.

The technical bit: Some camera phone flashlights are xenon flash tube - but most these days are LED-style lights. These are bright but the burst of flash lasts too long. This can cause blurry images if the subject is moving.

(left): Flash only. *(below):* brightness increased + flash

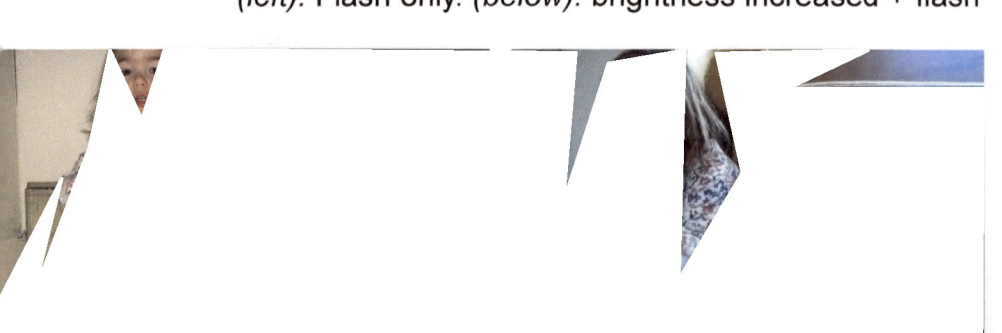

15

Use flash in daylight

Okay, I know I said don't use flash inside. And you're thinking: Now he's telling us to use flash outside! In daylight! This is madness!

Well, just hang on a minute. Hear me out. Using flash in daylight – bright, bright daylight – is one of the best things you will ever do. All proper photographers do it.

All you need to remember is that flash does not reach very far (especially on mobile phone cameras). But as you've already positioned the subject in the foreground (with you quite close by), the flash is perfect for illuminating them while your camera phone will usually automatically expose for the rest of the scene itself. The idea with this technique is to eliminate those images you have taken in the past where the background looks lovely but the subject in the foreground is a silhouette. The flash can also saturate the image and bring out the bright colours. Which can be good. It's almost easy, this.

You are essentially using fill-in flash here (and most likely no sticky tape).

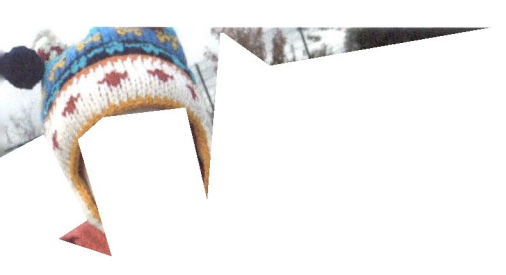

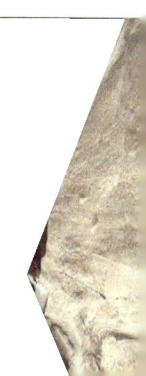

16

Get a better phone

This, of course, is the expensive option. Many of the best camera phones now cost more money than a mid-range digital slr camera.

But those DSLR's don't fit in your pocket. And you will use your camera phone more because it is always with you. Some professional photographers now shoot editorial images exclusively on mobile phones. Some photojournalists have found a way to make it work in certain situations and environments.

Here is a list of the best camera phones. Mind you, it is just a guide - new phones and upgraded models come out all the time. One thing worth noting, the cameras on iPhone 4s and below are rubbish.

The best camera phones

(in no particular order)

1 Nokia Lumia 1020

2 Apple iPhone 5 or higher

3 Samsung Galaxy S4

4 Sony Xperia Z or S

5 HTC One/HTC One X

17

Back up your images

Use automatic upload to a cloud (brilliant for when your phone gets stolen and the thief starts taking selfies). Or just copy files to your hard drive often. Phones get lost and they break. Either way, don't lose your images.

18

The End

And that's it. Thanks for reading this. A lot of effort has gone in to presenting some serious information in as short and easily-digestible form as possible. I hope it has worked for you. If it has or it has not, I love feedback. Either on social media @gazcook or via email gazcook@hotmail.com

If you would like to book me for yourself or your business (I do individual as well as group workshops) please get in touch. I live in Lancashire, England, but just love to travel (with my camera).

I have books available to buy on Amazon: bit.ly/GarryCookBooks

And I have a clunky self-designed website at gazcook.com where I publish all of my experiments in image making, storytelling, audio/imagery and video imagery.

Thanks

Garry Cook

January 2015

Those contact details again

You can engage with me on   email: gazcook@hotmail.com

Twitter @gazcook   Thank you for buying this

You can ask questions on   guide book.